# THE SORROW FESTIVAL

ERIN SLAUGHTER

"Erin Slaughter's *The Sorrow Festival* is an archive of transformations: the moment that a nest of verdant vines unfurls into choking overgrowth, the flesh that softens past ripeness into rot, the sting of shame that follows the pleasure of succumbing to a frivolous desire. In an effort to understand the tipping point at which one thing topples and becomes another, the poems in this lush collection look to the natural world, and to history, and to mythology. Seeking clarity, these poetic excavations more often reveal complex contradictions about love, desire, and obligation that are every bit as murky as the Florida swamplands where the work is set. *The Sorrow Festival* serves as a vital catalog of the constant uncertainties we all endure in exchange for the promise of intimacy, and the hope of stability."

—Jenny Irish, author of *Tooth Box*

"These poems are feral. They are omnivorous. They fuse the saccharine and the grotesque into a kind of emotional banquet—a place where you can't recall how you arrived, but you know you can't leave. This is a poet with one hand covered in blood and grease, the other impeccably manicured. *The Sorrow Festival* will make you feel hot and bothered, sad and giggly all at once, like a spell cast by a horny cave-dweller in a funeral gown."

—Nate Duke, author of *A Suit of Paper Feathers*

In *The Sorrow Festival*, Erin Slaughter renders a deft lyric of rememory. Here, in these lush and fervid poems, a woman transforms her grief and self within a borderland of surreal mundanity. This collection is alchemy and testifies to a woman's ability to emerge from a recursive past and thrive.

—Tanya Grae, author of *Undoll*

In this bountiful collection, Slaughter weaves a brilliant tapestry of lace and longing, and of guttural instinct silenced by circumstance. These poems extrapolate a violent inner world of transformation through language, recalling the loneliness and triumph of womanhood in a bellowing, youthful ache for something untouchable. They ignite the quiet forgotten moments of life with furious integrity. *The Sorrow Festival* offers no forgiveness for the poet or the reader, but instead, a wet mouth beckoning you awake, promising not to swallow.

—Lena Ziegler, co-editor of *The Hunger* and author of *MASH*

# CONTENTS

# Contents

I'll tell you
many different things have the ability
to glimmer and that is as much a reason
for joy as for terror

— Nick Sturm, *HOW WE LIGHT*

Don't die, summer
There are wolves among us
We promise to make more art

— Emily Kendal Frey, *SORROW ARROW*

# I

# Digging Teeth Out Of The Garden

## THE HEART OF THE WARRIOR IS A MOON-FACED THING

ready to strike out its own eye
with its own tusk. I once heard a myth
about a man who ate a planet full of cakes, stashed hunger
in his belly as if there were no reason
desire should be secret, & rode through the desert til he split

open in the sand. I noticed spring's edges
rotting today & I do not look
at my face in the mirror. Outside, graffiti on the dumpster reads:
*soften*. But last week my friend was walking down the street
& a stranger put his hands inside her

like her body was a duffle bag to rifle through,
searching for keys. St. Augustine,
in what we remember as history, thought nuns were lucky
to be raped because it taught them humility. He said
that in their pain they ascended closer to God
than the average person, which is not at all
the skinned-kneed truth of being stolen
from yourself. When I try to search his words,

all people are concerned with is the fall
of Rome, as if a country burning
didn't fashion itself from matches like these, striking off
solitary in the holy dark. Actually, it was an elephant,
not a man. The myth of an elephant

who wove serpents into a corset for his gluttony, wore
their stretched, scaled bodies, shameless. I read
that when an elephant breaks
away from manners to rampage its captors, they say
it has *gone ugly*. That man will never know the mouse-

sweetness in my friend's morning voice, how she can fall into sleep
on the least-forgiving surfaces. Still, sometimes I walk around outside
without underwear to remind myself the difference

between ignorance & trust. In the glorious swampland
I've accepted as my home, a man was recently arrested
for kicking swans in the head. Witnesses say he was laughing.

Here, the planes go all night & each creature squatting in the brush
is another set of teeth, sharpening.

## *NOTES ON UN-APOLOGY*

once I owned a wooden door
& a field of ice & I was big-hearted, gentle, prefaced
my friends' names with *sweet* & kissed them
on the cheeks. once a man called me *brilliant* & all I wanted
was to be his little wife. for him to trap me
in a wooden home, zip me up pretty, kiss
me in the kitchen while mushrooms screamed & withered
on the stove. I am beginning to think of the color green
as a last chance that has already passed & I'm sorry
to be so full of raining. but if I could carve a notch
into the lamp posts of this city for every person who said *home*
like it was a promise. we are fools & monsters, all of us, cobweb-headed
& waiting for rupture. once I met a man & his words
unearthed a softness that only comes from loam, from tilling
gently at a gravesite. sometimes we talk about weather
& sometimes we talk about feelings. sometimes
I worry I'm not looking for love, that I'm looking
for a religion to have sex with. in my mouth lives a bitterness
that could draw blood, & I'm sorry but two years I searched
for the river & when I finally found it, it was dead with its palms up.
I dipped my hands in its broken jaw & called it *sister*. I haven't spoken
to my sister in two years, a nurse in Texas
with a daughter & a cruelty that jingles
like silver on a charm bracelet. I want to tell you starfish, I want
to tell you dark orchids climbing the windowpane.
the moon would drown trying to drink up
all the things I want. I'm sorry you never learned
the recipe to my mornings. I still think of you when the sky shudders
& floorboards hush themselves to listen.

*FAILED ANIMALS*

My first hamster ate its babies
the first night in our house. From the cage
I peeled blue membrane, blubbery—that
was the year of the drowned
child from church, whose parents insisted
open casket to show last & finally

what they'd made. My mother taught him.
My sister, roundfaced, befriended
his great dane. His name is a secret
this poem hides vined up its shirtsleeves & swallows
as a fistful of keys. In the great deaths I've known,

there was no hospital, so like bleached barracks for wild cows
a hospital meant milk, meant birth, meant roaming
freedom's halls & pulling prayers out the chapel lockbox,
stealing nurses' redbull from a mini-fridge, any evidence
of our going to meat a long-tunneled eventuality. I admit

when I think bovine I think that college boy who referred
to the vagina as *sack full of cows' tongues,* & how much
we harvest from gentle creatures, bred & slaved—our cruelty
flings itself at the ozone like an old-fashioned movie
killer with plastic cheeks & a butcher knife. They say

no more seals or koalas soon. They say ravenous storms
& less turtles. It's trying to stop a raze of locusts
with useless tearful fury, then startling at the hungry click
of your own jaw's hinge. What I could tell you about my people,

my people who turned to honeysuckle
not out of sweetness, but boredom & desire
to dismantle something live that would not yelp.
That seasoned our unblemished legs with the copper
softball pitch. That I was a child, for no reason
glitter-thrilled that strangers identified me
feminine, as a hen must be when held

skirtless by its scaly legs before slaughter.
My people, ethanol perforating brains like hollows in nests.
My people, what are they but smoke & boom & gone.
My grandmother's house smells arsoned appliances,
my grandfather's books crushed mollusks between pages.
Some mice cannibalized in the neighbor's trailer bathtub

up the overlooking hill. That is a lie, those mice
were mine, my sister's. Two, like us, in their pyrex microcosm
on a corner desk buried by crayons & doll trash. Friends
in their only world, they ate one another & collapsed
in husks of the tiniest bone. It was our fault, our ark
of failed animals. We forgot about them. We had our own
bedrooms.

## HOW WE RECKON

A sister is a thing that burrows
just beneath the flesh & can't be burned
away by months of red leaves. She itches
brightly awful, a loose tooth
you can't bear to pull

My sister texts me
she is pregnant for the second
time, a boy, & I cry valleyed

under a friend's spawning
porchlight because this
is how we feed: on the ambulance
of sorrow strobing beneath skin

*Estranged.* To be remade
a lop-legged beetle in your own image
To uncoil from the umbilicus of a map

//

When the birds at my door
jingle their flimsy cloth & iron bell
as I'm on my way out
to the bar I am reminded

our dead father's ghosts, the ones
he said this string of birds is meant
to warn of, are always

just me, knocking around
the dark walls like a trapped rat

I sink to the smell of his bottled
spirit, crystalline rivers distilled
in potato blood. Nectar of clockwork,

every two years I consider sobriety;
admit I'm just looking
for another piece to shovel into light

//

October's the wolf month,
sprawling, a lovely
shallow knick in flesh

In the arms of a lover
who is not mine
I am a dirt child

I avoid the animal
of his eyeshine in the bluish dark,

wary the spell
of cotton that is conjured
if we lock eyes as he enters me

The distance between
his fingers form a red cradle
of thread where his phantom
partner tightropes like a wax
statue in a museum
I've never visited

Sister, I too have become vengeful
in my longing

for something other than the pit
of linen-pleated forgiveness

I find myself mother to red-pelted creatures
They rest their woeful muzzles
across my washingboard heart-
strings in the lush, palm-wreathed night

Their sweat sings: *It's past time*
*you bred something more*
*than coddled suffering. Hothouse*

*contracting your expanse*
*around blankness,*
*no flora gone squirrelly*

*in the submarine hull*
*of your belly*

/ /

My niece & now
nephew will grow
in the red cleft
of a gull's tongue,

in the state that demands
fistfuls of dust to span
its landscape, a state folks return

their dead to ripen in gowns
of the soil they birthed
from. The easiest state to hide
a body, gravity reversed
in a tomato field

/ /

Sister, when you are entered
by silences seeking a place
to mend

their wings, you recoil, sprout
fresh inmates, breed pithless
new gods

Sister, if you are hungry to unhusk
it is easy to forget the dark's
stinging bone. It is easy to blame a shadow
for its retractions

//

Miles & miles, you curl in a blanket
of cellar walls, dewy with futures
that stumble aimless as newborn foals

Our dead's eyes
grow large as the cold
hemisphere of a planet

& I promise to write more odes
to my uterus
It used to bring me dead things

like the neighborhood cat
laid a splayed
cardinal at the foot
of my bed

The beautiful organ
of it thrashed
against death, that excellent monogamist

## THE BEEKEEPER'S ABORTION

I dated a beekeeper that winter out of longing
for spring. Because the days were rough opals
circling a wound & I didn't care
what happened to me. Because his mutters
of *honey*—& thought perhaps to name
the breathing objects of this life in sweetness
would make a mouth taste sweet. I watched

him pour buckets of thick amber in a house
that smelled like someone's grandparents
left them too young, & this was the year
the last five men I'd fucked or loved were blue-
eyed, one long nightmare of wish-fulfillment & I stopped
calling myself vegetarian, though still told most people
I met that pigs have the consciousness of a human
toddler. New Years I'd resolved to eat less
animal bodies & consumed three bags
of pork rinds the following day. So I bite down

on the absolute freedom of failure, so a beekeeper
works his way inside me like a gardener tilling air into bloom
& my body opens without my permission. In his kitchen
was a black liquor bottle with another man's name
& I turned the label away while he kissed me.
The mattress on the floor collecting
frantic capillaries, frictionless sparks
hiving in my cricket legs

until the room began to smell of souring bodies.
His human name was Adam & he was the first man
I let come inside of me. Buzz pulsing
under my hips, the muffled thud of dead antelopes.
Frivolous loss of judgement, I admit

I am the embarrassing scriptwriter & costumer
of my own life, that in fearful delight I fantasized
a storybook grief that could become, at least,
this title—that it might take scalpel & suction
to hollow myself of him—& remembering
he had only daughters, their small hands
stained in ink, captives in a photo hidden
hastily in the crease of his bookshelf.

Remembering the first cold night I stopped
at the gas station & drove home with a bag
of beef jerky in hand, triumphant,
the not-quite promise of intimacy
dripping down my thigh.

## [NOT THESE WHITE PILLS LACED WITH SUN]

*after Rebecca Hazelton*

Nor humid winter's backyard, amber-rimmed sky that bled
its fanatical orchards without complaint. Terrible things have happened
                to better people on worse patches of grass. My 24th year I was

                        the prettiest abyss. Long chocolate ribbons of hair,
                beautiful & foolish in ways hard to forgive. The heart is truly
an embarrassing creature—not to claim anything was rotting
                in mine, only that it stank periodically,
as if mulling over its options. Whatever came first, the larvae or

eggwhites hurled over the toilet bowl before work.
                No perimeter of barbed wire to take note of, no
                        guards of the heart patrolling its silence or hooligans
skateboarding through the night to jump its gate, oblivious

to desire's opulent chokehold. There were no dogs
lapping the edges of its refusal to soften, just expository barking
                heard through the fallopian tunnel of a conch shell. I promised
a god I spoke to only through bedlinens
I would not allow myself another drink
                til after New Years', o with all the lounging

                        that floral-printed sofa, suckling bottles of Jack I buried
in my landlady's garden, blackmailed the deer, anxieties like mice
climbing the sun-blinds, pleaded apologies only to the ocean
                for how little of it I came down from the hill to touch
                        without some ampulla of blue-veined vinegar
                        to sweeten me on living; a ransom to coax
                                me to the streets, the shoreline, the quiet colonies keening

for an execution's stillness. I wouldn't call this regret. I have slept
full-bellied on my own decrepit floorboards &
                                        woke hopeful, believing hope

is not the fray-feathered goose it presents itself, not
          the small-armed grieving beast
holed up beneath memory's
                         raspberry surface.

Undone by no beloved hands on sopped glasses. Nothing darling &
beheaded.
Not a thing possessing any neck at all.

## *INEVITABLY YOU WILL KNOW PEOPLE*

who very bad things happen to / & you will not know how to help
them / & your hands will be only your hands / not any moonstained
sky worth speaking of / think of your own hypothetical husband
dying / suddenly on a train in Canada / & ache for someone you
haven't known / who nonetheless haunts your blood & time / like a
flimsy spent thing / wading in / the blue & secret rust of it

// /

the rust & faithless blue of / time that long hallway of nosebleeds /
my friend's young husband served three tours / in Afghanistan & was
pulped / by a bus in Dallas now she has a life / of wedding photos
bathed / black & white she was young, beautiful / she is young still /
& beautiful & will never be / whole again where are you I am afraid
/ you might be on a plane is someone with you

// /

our hands are only our own / not clouds or shovels worth speaking
of the aching / acceptance: others get to choose / how to spend their
lives as if there are years / like pretty silver / pieces limitless as if we
aren't a gust / of salt a pile / of wind love makes ghosts / of the loved
& someone when we touch them sees / our fingers slip past / the
borders of their skin & shudder

// /

forgive me for I am not a patriot / of human living I have pledged
allegiance / to the abrasive beauty of the plum tree & a mouthful
/ of air splitting the lungs / at various times have continued to be
alive only out of guilt / for my mother my best friend or my cat /
can sometimes force myself / to eat only by the knowledge that my
emptiness / makes another suffer / I have ground my teeth to dust
with a love-loaded gun to my head

// /

with a love-loaded gun to my head / today I heartbroken swept the hair of a woman / whose lungs sprouted black gardens / & outgrew her / whose lungs charred / like southern churches & so is shucking her body / away from the world inch by inch, thankful / for another day clothed in flesh / beside her flesh-trapped husband she has begun / to practice prying off the world like opalescent scales / vanishing herself from / her wonderous gutted & only life

/ /

gut-wrenching wonderous this strange hot planet / keeps no sentiment we are / sediment shedding selves still / I'd set fire to this metaphor / to hear is someone with you do your days / trickle out like nosebleeds / & what if desire is a corrosive thing that clings / to none of its words & what about people who don't make it / to the scene in the starlit tunnel / where the music swells / it's enough to pry me from my cold dead grip / on dignity to say here that I hope / there will still be some time, some glimmering morsel, some ember of time left for us

## ELEGY FOR RECORDING THE LIGHT

> with *"Victor Jacquemont Holding a Parasol, 1865"* & a line from
bell hooks

Do you ever get sad thinking all the dogs
in old paintings are dead? More helpless
        than the past is the bruise that carves
it into canvas & the root of *martyr*,

I learned, is *witness*. So I practice saying no
to dusk's orange heel, poised above
        my throat. As if existence has a bloodthirst
for testimony. As if stillness is a eulogy

I'm working up the bravery for.
*Contemplating death leads us*
        *back to love.* It's not that the dark
is thicker, but that in the meteoric

hours under a soup's-ladle
of Orionids, I'm embedded with need
        to pass sunflower atoms from my tongue
to your tongue. There are so many people

I will never see old: Most. My father
hiding in the blackberry field
        lacing the sun to his ghost boots. After
you tell me about the island mangroves,

I gift you a jar of blackberry jam
from my grandmother's land & remember
        Monet's admission that while
watching someone he loved

die, he spent up the time analyzing
the pigments in her eyelids, deciding
        how to paint them. We can only learn
so much from squatting in the dirt

with capillaries hung like dried roses
to preserve in the shroud
            of pages. I'll spend a life failing
to befriend the fear that all of this glows

& ends: a faint slash of tenderness
            before the sorrow festival.

## LATE SEPTEMBER EARLY OCTOBER HEMORRHAGE

there's a witch grave in Tallahassee altar      for
tea-thimbles pennies      I tell you her wedding
date carved           into the pillar sandwiched
between birth      & death & 100 years to the day
before my own parents married      you glance at
the sky like you're waiting for a cloud      to bruise
you god-fisted      these days I am remarkably
sunlit absorbing        & considering tenderness a
verb      hold breath to walk past a cemetery find
wishing instead a collapsed lung      a word loses
meaning the more you imagine      how it would
move in front of you      sincerity unbearable as
squinting      into the wet open throat of summer
people like us aren't looking      for happiness but
these trees might be enough      Pisces moon &
sentimental fern shadow      burn away clean as
brushfire *nobody loves a city nobody loves      what can't
love them back*      but if I sit still      enough & let my
voice play painter      in the cave      if I'm hermit
& gin-soaked it's all language      of possession
the only difference      between selfishness & love
is who gets to walk away      from what      I tell you
I stumbled on a wedding photo was shocked
to see my parents holding each other      's gaze
my mother's eyes      fearsome blue      & wide how
finding that grave      was the thriftshop version
of a magic I always meant      to get around to
feeling & you tell me      as a kid you were made
to stuff poison into meats      feed to dogs      on
the other side of the fence      not knowing why
on the other side of the page some boy in some
lake      floats in the nailed-shut window      of
what his heart doesn't know      will leave him
unscathed      the difference between empathy &
fidelity is who presses what words      into whose
skin who pretends      to or to not swell with
narrative who carries story      like a clung rot
tooth      nobody can bear to pull

## HOLDING THE LOOSE BONES CLOSE

My mother the morning of her surgery lies
in a room where I am not

The angelbones her hair is
tied fraying in hospital cotton

There are plans to remove
the knot of gut from her throat
where it has climbed & come to rest so she can not
          eat & sometimes breathing
feels like so much heartbreak / I imagine metallic choirs of fingers

itching their way into freckled motherskin, doctors with hands
like chariots, like
gravediggers, like men who have come to take something

          & promise lack will make you whole

*//*

The morning I do not know
is the morning of my mother's surgery I dream
following her through small-town dusty streets

dragging behind me an antique white rocking chair
she will not let me put down or give away, says
it will only be a little further      to where we are going

As a child I chewed holes in the sleeves of my sweaters

We lived in a broken home but by that
I just mean the oven handle
was hanging off its hinges & there were dents

        in the doors nobody asked about
One dent in particular,

        she was holding the baby / When the bottle flew / Clipped
        her hair / She could have left him then

        They are happy now / I believe / Their ceiling fan carved
        in the shape of a fish

*//*

I do not know my mother
will refuse surgery, will choose to live

> in pain a little while longer for hope
> is a wildbright thing that nests like a dog
> giving birth under the house or a cat
> hiding away to die & I drive

to work that morning, passing
ads for touchless breast exam & car wash
all the songs on the radio about learning
not to trust someone who could love you or pretend to

My father, my sister
with silver in her veins—
> I want to ask

when does a fish hook caught in the netting of the heart
become a bear's claw clamped over it

> This gouging, an inheritance
> stuffed with tissue paper & wet yellow yarn

*/ /*

When she looks at pictures of my father, dead now
after the powerlines drunken cut

the beloved stuffed doll that never spoke again after he threw
her out into the snow / When we were only babies / How much she
hid

sparkled shards of if not pain than pretty
hurt things / Her whole red smile a promise:

> *one day you will be a hole like that & you will learn to sing within it*

//

My mother kept her children's baby teeth
in a plastic bag hoarded in her bedside
dresser drawer so she could sleep
dragonlike guarding our innocent bones

> The poet writes of burying
> her children's teeth in the garden

One of these strikes me a more beautiful ritual: inviting
something precious & impossible to grow, a letting go

the other: a gluttony
of memory / A rootless nostalgia that rots
from the way it is loved

I want to believe I am free enough to be
the first kind of person but I know

> I would end up digging those teeth out of the garden at night

holding the loose bones close
to my face,

> as if they could speak again

# II

# RIVER

on my father's death day I do not write I wear a dress
earrings feel as if it matters the air a ripe wet lung as
it always is it rains as it does daily I do not tilt my face
towards or away fall asleep hair smelling cigarette &
soft ash tell a stranger at the bar *if I have to drink another
gin & tonic this week I'll scream* I order another my throat
writhing quiet like a mouse on the edge of python's
teeth delighted in proximity to a thing with the ability
to slice I do not write do not tell my friends except the
day before & day after I say *it was*

*my father's death day & it will be* I catalog men who do
not love me their voices scrubbed from their words
monuments I visit daily as if sentences are not expired
& stone as if I will catch them growing new branches
& climb flowering to elsewhere there is no grave to
visit my father is ashes which means he is nowhere I
remember his phone number do not call it or want
to startle who's on the other line & call this kindness
though secretly

every six months or so confirm it's disconnected plug
flaccid hanging from the wall who'd want to take
residence in a murdered man's ear who on this earth
can wrangle responsibility for their one regretful mouth
the night before I tell a boy say *tomorrow is my father's
death day* we say other things too stolen cigarette from
a sad man in a booth my skirt awry smeared gardenia
thighs it's summer still august & always its neon-petaled
violence he asks me to suck his cock in the backseat of
my car I bargain for his lips but take neither wake hazy
& ecstatic I have so much dignity I can barely believe it
that I escaped intact

when my self had any choice in the matter I've made
carnivals of splitting my flesh wide as spectacle to see
what insects come hovering the scar line sleep alone
dream I am a literal queen wearing a literal crown
the whole fucked country bracing themselves to be
pummeled by motorcades of desire I'm sorry & I'm
not on the anniversary of death I'm wearing red it was

an accident another gin & tonic I have grown so much
to love it here

& cry now only on Sundays & when stoplights sprawl
the wet street like roadkill rending garments of
manufactured light my friend buckles his knees to meet
me at eye level there is an infant in this bar who will not
remember us I glance at his hands my chest opening
around a stone there is no name for

& laughter no talk of endings how they are so much
beginnings a single unsightly morning played on
various sets struggling to get it right & losing to feral
noise stumbling joyous through bush & mud & foreign
asphalt sometimes there are trees which make a
difference I am trying to get it right this time so speak
to me of swineherds owned by ill-intentioned valleys
of the bloodclot algae that blooms the drinking supply
for miles tendons neatly filed beneath the skin another
gin & tonic I have no secrets have never I wretch them

up whole like fish my father was an alcoholic he was
probably other things but time is a river that corrodes
all but the pillars memory & the unseemly dead of us
swept like leaves from the street never met a body of
water so unafraid of forgetting if we have the same
blood if your blood is my blood how much of our
blood is poison he thought when he died he was leaving

a wife new cobbled future stretched out if not a
field a standard sidewalk maybe with dawn splashed
like spoonfuls of orange sherbet I once got so high
convinced myself I wrote every Bon Iver song once
played ukulele for beings I loved more than my own
organs & thought us heaven once loved one person &
learned a song he hummed I still remember the chords
though can't remember his voice only the polished
shape of his fingernails that he opened me & I flooded

childlike glittering agony entered & I clenched around
it like a bleeding rabbit around a hole in the dirt that his

eyes were windows blue & lit with no geography glass
doors leading to nothing that he lived a mirror was of
the mountains & far away now streaked with red dust
some other life I tell people I will die young

tell people I love they will die very old & withered
imagine time an eroding storm around the jewel of
enduring eyeshine gnaw on the song of it for pleasure
here's a secret never uttered if you are someday
someone in an old photograph I am grateful to have
known you I swear this fistful of bone I will cry until
there is no salt to be hunted

from your story a song that would split the living sear
delicate maps from palms I was harvested from shells
of torn-down truck stops migration a luxury only river
I'd known the roadside ditch I fled to at twelve glass
fractures & shoelaces gritty 7-up bottles & coors I was
found of course & dragged by my arm from the pit
tearful begged to scrape new existence from that grave
of shard & mud some towns are small & living is tedious
*sorrow* is not the right word *redemption* is

too valorous & I am seasick of *forgiveness* I would just
like to say that I finally found a collection of thorns
to harm me in ways I've only longed for at the bar a
friend says *you have a face that makes me want to tell you all
my secrets* I laugh as if I am the goddamn river itself as
if any body silt stone wet bank of thrumming motion a
human would choose

to drown in whatever is burning anyway is not burning
here the river is a place people croon loneliness they
call it their own names & sometimes it answers a crater
for boys to splash dazzling in their long-limbed hate
the thing about these boys they are never surprising
always alive inside their skin smile a corsage pinned at
the corner of their mouth begins to rot before you even
take it home but oh how pretty in a florescent drug store
kind of way & girls too wishing to translate freedom
into the next hungry moment as if by swallowing could

hoard a vial of earlobe eyelash instant of dizzy sweat as
if there is any door inside us we can nail shut that flood
will not lick open for example I would like to share a
meal with you without hibernating

inside my organized bones or choking down these
burdened orchards the river has no secrets like this
unless if you call secret what churns beneath the surface
poised to tug strangers to its center & if you only float
you will only ever feel it love you but why when to be
split like sugared bark so gently in the current's womb
even an animal would not bother a death so fragrant
yes people have died

at the river submerging their necks open eyes rinsed
blank their hands their hands an afterthought hair
tangled as tillandsia yes even some ugly core of water
craves memorabilia to buttress the ravine of days &
lunar dark to ransack words like a pile of loose matches
what can they do who will language save or shelter exile
now

from river its aches of sun & moss-itched charm
tonight I wish to be a dull man on a porch drinking
plain American beer a man who has never thought
about hands beyond what they can & can't make
happen staring into the potato-dense night trees laden
with screeching with my birthday card every letter my
grandmother includes information addresses phone
numbers & names petitions so the woman who killed
him stays

barred up & barren-armed I lie & do not write them two
weeks before this year's death day I turned 25 alone on
a southeastern beach & hallucinated flock of wrinkles
what cliché I wore a fancy dress to dine with no ghosts
stumbled in humid dark & forced cobblestone my
grandmother says he was her small buttoned baby says
of his wife who killed him *monster* yet for months they
slept beside one another without incident I wonder if
she watching him breathe woke to hear him choke on

sleep & felt fond I ask

no one if I were to divorce this grief it would wrack
me bloodspilt on some suburban carpet too make of
my skull the same unrelenting doorway if grief was a
tablet that dissolves instead of dormant virus singing
its lunatic sorrow in the bloodstream fear one day I will
again love someone something one day I will survive
to love no one wanting nothing & if the day my lover
comes home smelling of embankments iron-drenched
mud & a salt belonging to ether if he reveals a hand
not an altar

built for absence or for to clench around absence call it
sustenance call us starved if I beg him to scar me some
evidence of him there & real if he gestures only to the
crippled oak if the revolver at my neck

is to be expected & his eye a cyan apology what then
marks this waterlogged tongue mangled manic life-
scarred interesting at parties if healing is a flower so
simple with glory it has never even dreamt the back of
my throat

# III

# Land Of The Rootfisted

## THESE WEEKS ARE EXCEEDINGLY FLORAL

Have I told you how the trees here scream all night, the spiders
that crawl up my skirt if I sit long enough
to look up & see stars. Frenzied frequency
of cicadas, on a blanket in the yard
we construct new constellations entirely eel-based.

Bearded men in a dive bar line up to watch *Jeopardy!*
on the small yellowed TV chant ritual of beer-breath
nostalgia *what is crocus what is yarrow* I ask
the great beyond *can you help me spell "apprehensive" without error.*

Pocketknife graffiti sketched into the bathroom wall
tells me *I'LL MISS THIS TOWN* before I even have a chance to
though I know of course that shipwreck's coming, string music
slicing sweet & sharp through projected distance.

The first thing I laid eyes on when I came
to consciousness this morning was a video
of a black bear & baby deer, just staring, sniffing
curious harmless. When they grow older such creatures
will murder each other in teeth.

When you start talking about lilac trees & mountains
as more than mountains are I want to tell you that even before
your landlord plastered the flimsy brick steps I'd never tripped
on them, they've never done me wrong. Elsewhere the night

becomes an ambulance under non-committal
oil-spill clouds some unsupervised valve
near my heart must be leaking
engine smoke tonight I am glad to know your chest
is only a secret windstorm.

Brightening spine in the orifice of an oak trunk, tree
in a gutter of field, & who is filled
by this, does our city have a tongue, location?

Forgive me the typo, I did not mean to write
*"our ghosts are* 'wood' *for all eternity"*

but I do believe we are light from the same tree
have alighted from the same knotted branch
lit from the same branch down.

## THE COOL GIRL FAÇADE BEGETS ITS OWN LAYER OF ANIMAL GRIEF

Twice-daily hurricanes leave Spanish moss matted to telephone
poles like lake-stained hair of drowned girls who what shame were
born

with the right kind of bones & moderate amounts of flesh
so consideration of isolated death felt genuinely optional

Watch the sky bleed messy on the backlit
beacon of the A-frame Whataburger a rosegold mansion embedded

in weeknight slumbering greenery & oil rags
tossed in the road mistook for pillaged lumps of fur

Florida is grieving out loud like a teenager with a belly ring
smudging careless blooms of ash into her parents' bedroom carpet

a wracked girl more dirt than blood more knuckle
than plumage a girl who spits out any food she bites & aches never

If I'm going to pretend there's ever been a time when wandering
the grounds of a public graveyard isn't where I felt safest

I'll need a city like this with a fist & slicked-up teeth
a shatterglass sunlight that grabs

by the hair & pulls hard more frightening than sexy
swoons eerie as muffled flashlight through a sunken cruise ship

Four nights ago a baby lizard orange & translucent as a condom
scurried across my foot on bathroom tile

& took shelter in the unseamed edge
of the wall the next morning its tiny corpse

fetal fingernails unformed snout & paw was hardening
upside-down in a spider's web on the porch

There's a reason why women in old movie posters
are looking far off into mysterious distance

To know that someone else had just finished sacrificing
a finch at my altar would you kiss me then all liquorvoid

Dinosaur's egg eye
cracked granite & fishbone all fucked through it

Would you scar me cypress bark & swallow longing
Lukewarm glimmering flock of lies it's alright I can take it

I've watched that space between wood planks grow furry
as cotton candy watched that lizard's remains go rot & chrysalis

suspended in amniotic sunlight I've stumbled in late avoiding
the lunar glow of it dense & unflinching in the dark

I'm going to let my hair grow long again
spread corkscrewed in the grass like weeds

rootfisted & starved for belonging
Gonna take the backside of a broom & let the webbed corner

reclaim its cottonthirst absence. It's time to cut that creature's body
down.

## NO HORSES

Because giving pleasure is less vulnerable
than receiving. Like animals in the underbrush
scuffing for hours in the barren dirt
for fruit: perhaps we seek in sacrifice
a kind of safety. That mirage
sealed with ore, to be *loved*, meaning
*hollowed until solved*. & measured
in penitent seasons: sallow in my shame
costume, gnawing the chicken bones
hidden in the side of the mattress he refuses
to crawl to. I've spent a life testing how many
men I could stuff in my mouth until one swam
their way to the laughing wound. Or said *thank you*.
Or fed me dense bright spoonfuls
of salt. Who taught us love is an arrow
whose harsh jaw we aim at ourselves. No horses
prize splitting their hooves this way. A girlhood sealed
by deprivation's bronze tongue gives compassion
a chemical taste. Silverfish, choose yourself
a sunken thing. It is worse to survive someone kind.

## HURRICANE FRAGMENTS

the irrelevant     deprivations they
did nothing I was not whole my mouth still
my own

I am truly a ragged
woman     freckleborn
under this paint

//

they can smell it
on you that you're craving
yourself a place     for them to drown
their swollen tangle of felled branches   they
smell it     animal contained pretty
self-container help him     become
more perfectly regardless but maybe

he will find you pretty maybe you are someone

or so he tells     bestows
like a glittering golden fig all
that acceptable personhood     licks it
into your palm snapped
powerlines that tongue     thank you thank you
what affirmation trophy sewn into me

/ /

shaved slippery little lizard tricked some man
into driving me out of town      Tallahassee
evacuates its poets smell of gulf-rot

scavenge like a mouse tortilla
chip crumbs moment alone      in the kitchen
when I get back to Florida gonna slurp syrup
from felled tree debris

stop mining scraping begging
at the site of what they will
& will not give      a rodent
jostling its cage for improbable
few drips of water      leave them

a little ragged-skinned      feel
like a fat speckled frog in a bathtub
but like I could still trick      some boy
into loving me or feeling
saved      which in some circles
of my heart are the same      you never
claimed there were no predators      here

*//*

hurricane what hurricane saw a pine
uprooted like pulled teeth meat gristle
still attached     my chest a darkness
room no furniture

always another
trauma ready to loose you
from your shell of meat you just
haven't met it yet

men are not taught
in the same way to cultivate
the lingered gardens of their sorrow

//

a man texts me to make sure
the storm didn't consume
me how often have his words pulled
me from consumption self
or otherwise     says *so glad*
*you're okay* pairing
my lockjaw heart with a bird's beak the kind
you find suddenly     detached
in the road
                          watch the wound wilt slow
as possibility watch the sunlight
                          open quiet into wound

//

I have split my gums praying to the god of trajectory

I am looking now for someone
          who will hurt me in the ways I desire to be hurt

*//*

small rabbit sacrifice chews
cries from fear     the purity
of it a blunt object singing
to the skullframe fist to nose     scavenge
what bones are left after the storm
            solemn-mouth he doesn't need
to open to consume     dustlight barrels
of lakewater tinted     won't be
missed or questioned is this freedom

to be as you are     ceilingless blameless
& wildebeest     does he feel

more animal than anything animal
caged     in all this streaming bloodvine

//

I appreciate a man
who searches every corner
of the house the first time he comes in      interrogating
each photo     thumbtacked
above the desk

all bodied-up in the way I like I wonder
            will he dent me will he extract the shrapnel

I've grown adult in the sense
that I've found what makes me
feel safe      & accepted
its flaws

//

today morning mirror promise I'll wear
my hair up the way he likes      wear
perfume compliments      so much spent
becoming an amalgam of men's
revisions      body just another costume
for theatrics      convenience

yesterday allowed
myself to clench
around my hunger      & today my collarbones
are jewels

sticking out my tongue
at fruit flies      swarm
my face      let the feral
muck of self build
over me like a blister

//

N says don't trust a man
who brings a hatchet
to a campground he'll try
to chop down something living     don't trust anyone
who wants to build
a homestead out of some
extension of himself     I won't

//

so lightbreak you are & what monster to the sky
all this electricity lake
            river to the sky of bone
    love has broken
            my broken the moss

sunlights out of me like worms

//

dark Mississippi porch I held a steakknife
to the sky & begged
a reckless man to slice me    I actually
did that    All my desires
slipping from their sockets

## SPLINTERWOOD SOLSTICE

I fall asleep thinking about the cruelty of structures, dream of chauffeuring the dark & wake too cold for socks. day breaks against my nose, breaks skeletal, I take a mosquito's only chance at life with the pit of my elbow. return to my body, find it overgrown with thistle & barb. bury a penny tails-up in mud & wish for a new bloodstream. I miss you fierce like oilfields; I cut out my own tongue. your hand is memory, fiberglass, proximity. my fingernails blue themselves silly in rain, descendants of my mother's in the grocery. yes, need is a gravel succubus, so I tell myself I don't. you are nectar for the solstice, but I will not anymore become a house inviting ghosts. I will, for now, take the porcelain that is given, fashion a thorn crown out of white pine & simple movements. in my castle of dry brown bone, we are safe from knowing one another. I am locked doors & open windows & I am coming to terms with this. I will contort my legs to splinterwood, cocoon in the hot wet husk of trees that veil their arms & linger light. I will burrow myself in ice & pray it staves off future, rot, & flies.

## *I HOPE MY SALT LAMP IS A WEEPING DEITY*

& not evidence that my house
is sprouting a fever. I wake to find the base
leaky with saline, a puddle of wettened shelf, & send
L a picture of the flood, calling it *prophet*
with a question mark. She informs me
*prophet* is the wrong word; a prophet needs language—but what
is this lamp but a mouth: rock hollowed of light
& slobbering. I have pressed my tongue
to this stone in prayer for luminescence, for living
salt not siphoned from my own skin. I live
in Florida & had to turn the heater on today
for the first time since I've lived in Florida.
I used to love winter until I fell in love

under a funeral of Christmas lights, childhood's
ghost flooding from my overripe lips in mist—pleas
to the universe that never came true but propelled
me to Florida where I live untethered
to anything but my own plastic worship
of THE TREES. THE TREES meet me
where I am when I am lonely. I am lonely

& just learning how to say *I'm lonely* & not mean it
as a placeholder for the other absences
a noun leaves. I'm sitting on the porch
steeped in the ordinary human sadness
of not getting what I hoped for. After your hand on my neck
I felt so barefaced & linen. Now I'm stuck
hoarding words like choirs of expensive ants.
There are people near & far away
who have unspoken agreed to pass through this life
with me / isn't it enough / why can't I stop

talking about THE TREES, their haunted glitter
swirling like old pennies in my head. As if a taste of metal
at the back of the mouth means I can be salvaged
at the hands of someone I have yet to meet & if I present
my body as sacrifice I can finally walk away from it. I moved

to Florida to burn, molting magenta blooms, the summers
smothering every want with a wet open palm.
Like a birch switch. Like a kiss. I tell L, *I am*
*almost certain I will die alone*
*shriveled to the bone & huddled close*
*to a magnolia* TREE. There's still no way to get at
what I'm trying to get at, nothing to make up for the fact

I want to capture every purple flower
& hold it hostage in my throat. That I once believed monarchs
could live whole lives at my hairline
& showers did not make me sad & I was not afraid
of how much I have grown to love the blowfish,
taxidermied, hollowed into a lamp
hanging over the bar in wait for someone
to name him. This is a partial list of things
I would have once called suffering—how little
difference between noticing the details of anything
& loving it recklessly. The foolish heart

marching in all its birdsong & burgundy glitter
to stand in front of the firing squad. Everything today
feels bigger than the passing series of clouds
that shaped it. Aware even now I am choosing
which parts to remember, your words with their tiny
apologetic hooks of hope, the pattern of rain
falling across your skin & my desire
to show you how light never stops moving. If this secret
is a book of dark orchids in the archive
of our inevitable human hearts, it's nothing
new to say that I scraped my knees raw
on the sand kneeling over your body, that both
the wounds I did & did not ask for are shedding

to reveal new skin. I ask L, *Do you think it's possible*
*to be horny for poetry?* I am so tired of *mouth*,
trying to translate its meaning which has nothing to do with incisors
cheekflesh or the wily slide of tongue. For every hour lust paces
in its basement prison, there is a lost, feral possum inside of me

surviving very quietly. Everyone has agreed
the audience is tired of hearing about *the body*,
*the body*, but there was something
opening in mine, heaving like a litany
of cows giving birth in the pasture of night.
A TREE knows: *you've got to feel every follicle*
*of these painfields.* Says: *fold into the flooding.*
I hope someday to say out loud to anyone: you
touched me & touched me & touched me
& I was made better for it.

## ARS POETICA AS ELEGY

This morning 13 people were murdered
in the 311<sup>th</sup> mass shooting this year & you tell me
      you feel adrift like Shelley seducing the sea
to drown him & I tell you to go to the park

to watch ducks living out their days
in feather-cluster communities
      Because what else can be done, our country cleaves
itself into wounds that never quite capsize

the muscle but leave us disfigured
in dreamscape    A light
      smatter of public tearfulness & we try harder
to peek over the barricades of ourselves, to open our faces

to strangers but we are still fox-mawed
beneath these tender masks,
      gnawing our paws
in the silent soup of dirty-floored apartments

So I look to the words for guidance but every noun
is seraphim delirious in elegy
      every adjective a smear of pigment the rain
has swiftly siphoned from our skin

When Brathwaite wrote about a widow
of the fallen towers in flames frantically grasping
      at death's confetti in case
her husband was in the dust, *the gentle*

*liquid iris language of their prayers* revealed
how intimately water knows our thirst & is fine
      without us    The Shelley of myth who died
with Keats in his waterlogged pocket

& hot-breathed Mary forbidden to attend
the funeral, to flood with farewells at the fish-
      eaten remains of her love's
home, would be unsurprised

that this has become another poem
about the grief we feed to the river & the dread
            when it washes up at our feet on some other bank
Siken wrote that we can throw our sadness

into the river but we'll still be left
with our hands, & I wish
            I could show you the lists of words, the hours
spilling from my cupped palms as I cling

to collecting moments in petri dishes & hoarding
in jewelry boxes, as if sewing stories into the seams
            of skirts & sweaters will turn
these wire-strung vowels into people

who will love me or at least need
something    What potential homes have I discarded
            to follow toxic streams of alphabet
across this country's fissures

What can we recover in a series of symbols
created from our foolish hopeful fumblings
            in the dirt    Franklin wrote every blank page
as an elegy but she meant

something tangible, she meant the bodies in the streets
Every ode & elegy is unloosed flooding & you must open
            your lungs to the griefwound    Noun
an absence & adjective the flesh

blown open around it    We get to choose
what silt is lost to the river, which stones
            to throw back & which to pocket
for moments heavier than the hunting of salt

## INHERITANCE

to be human is to be peopled by loneliness / to carry loneliness

  like a stillborn city inside you / which is to say I lost my father

young / & flung my mother's name into a nest of sleeping vermin

  tossed the concept of my child's body to a pit of snakes / rather than rely

on breath to strangle it / I keep a copy of the book of the dead

  between my arm & my pillow / ink-blacken each name

stare in the craven dark so long / they all begin to look like mine

  to stumble hateful & blind / to share my shadow like a pool float in the restless

waves of night's crazed anchor / a bruise is the blood howling

  like a kennel of dogs behind a closed door / & each day is a page in a long

book of endings / every brazen touch a book of leavings

  there must be a way to know a heart from the inside / & forgive its unruly tunnels

its failings to teeter the edge / between sheltered & swallowed / to live

  without context is to live like granite shifting / oblivious as wood

before the saw's teeth / every stranger is a collection of cartilage

  & marrow with undefined intention / every place you have felt loved in

is another person's grave / which is to say love is a boneless room

  where the hands stutter & are reborn finally

as lanterns / where we come together / where we sink in

  innocent as breadknives

## *AT THE LOCUST FORK OF THE BLACK WARRIOR RIVER*

*after the 2019 Georgia & Alabama abortion bans*

I dig thumbprint graves, lay charred
        yarrow beneath the slash pine

                In dreams    No, in past
                            selves

        A controlled burn ruptures
the sky    a milk-
              crust bruise outside Biloxi

        My childhood closet was stuffed

with redheaded babydolls
              named for pieces of the body
        that start with R—

Ligaments
        The less-publicized bones

              Road & more road

        catching its tongue on the blood moon
            Supermoon

Orange & misshapen as a clot

                  40 minutes northwest
            of the room where my lover hovers
              me    a swinging lantern

People say women are sieves
        who must take what is given

                  That windless river grief
                laughs    gushes forth

as the pregnant women exodus
     to roadside ditches to eat
red clay with their hands     waterlogged

ballerinas stumbling in the rust-

      stained mud

         & with blood
         comes a sadness:

How free I remain

## (THE BILLBOARD CLAIMS) CAGED TIGERS LIVE LONGER IN LAFAYETTE

though still die & are memorialized
as wooden trailer, sun-lashed plastic
effigy. Below the overpass, alligators play their skins
accordions in mud. The sky opens up
like the descending cumulus tooth

of a hyena, & B & L backseat explain
the rain-patched sun: *the devil*
*is beating his wife*. Roadside, the sickly
oracle eye of the snakebird continues
hatching mayflies it can't tongue away.

//

We stop to see the camel
at the tiger-themed truck stop gnaw
the chain link, & imagine ourselves teenage
girls in that town, shuttling buckets of gray
horse meat through the grate on Friday night,
itchy with hope a particular cowlicked boy
might join her. The zygote that falls out of you
in this Louisiana gas-station bathroom
is a non-event; women countenance death
on the regular, bloom & rot a pendulum
in the grave of each our hips. *Miscarriage*
a freer girl might write & be called
sentimental—a pet name to indulge
the spot where rusted hook atrophies
the slack corner of her lip, pulls taught
a hollowed, sexy grin. You've anyway seen
at twelve the backroads coyote hovering
a carcass who believed perhaps it was
his favorite. And perhaps it was.

//

The story of tonight: we spend it
poisoning ourselves in all the fun ways.

N debunks the fallacy of heart
as open window while the half-drugged panther
night lacquers its teeth with zeroes.

In Florida you caught a habit for teasing flames
at bridges; sob later in the dregs
of coastal stoplights. Lafayette, you add a few
more to your vast graveyard of hatchets.

//

Tell B you've never been to those parties for boiling
arthropods in piles, but if a pair of reeling black eyes
sought you from a distance you'd pluck the creature
from its mass crypt, make of it companion; in secret,
bite its underbelly & accept whatever's there.

As in: any steady hand makes you twist, split
for Appalachian nothing-towns to perform
preemptive mourning. As in: what is the difference

between wanting a person & wanting the pain
that furnaces out of you under their cock-
eyed affection, unselves you a crumbling empress.

L says anyone can skin a rabbit clean
using just their hands—make a forked slit,
pull.

//

crimson flower without a moon     evicts the wraith from its driftwood fort

anatomy you are good at abandonment     as a child I wandered

into a cornfield got lost     mites carouseling in my bra     welted cut

through     to sirens on the other side     no I ran

into that toasted mouth surrender     my town lurked

breathing heavy stalks     the albino owl's

eyes     reflected the floor of a squatter's backwoods

cabin I never     left I never left     o that my lungs or any red word

could change me     the way this town's men speak

of wives as trowels & white violets unsnarl from trees to slime

the sidewalk     what is it about longing as a permanent state makes a girl

blind horny for burial     call me succulent queen in the harem of thirst

feathered eyelid slumbering in hot silk python gut

I wanted horses breathing kinetic in the plaster

I do not want to be another sweetness the bayou shucks open


*//*


Under hawkshadow, N drives until
the false nests that bauble Floridan trees
light you somatic. Somewhere, a person you could love
is uprooting succulents with the pronged side
of a hammer. Horizon pinking pine
bark, hog ponds, the slow-sinking villages
whose rotting curbs we cruise with starryeyed glee.

We will someday join the bestiary
of this sallow marshland—lie in the basement
valley, quilted in stringy mushroom, & forget
to rise. The tiger who crawls away to sleep in wombs
of burial will tell his old & lonely dreams
& we will listen, pillared.

# IV

# GULF EPISTOLARY

Dear P:

There's nothing new to say about the ocean, that grotesque centipede. Its ugly, sloshing prayer— which is the noise of us, and is us. In the new year, my hot water heater grinds itself lukewarm so every shower feels like penance for the body's eagerness to claim dirt as kin. I admit I've been avoiding you, the way anyone avoids looking at the deep center of a canyon. Absence becomes an object in itself, a kind of optical illusion. Today in class, I told my students: *You could've been a flower or a marmot or a hot dog cart, but you are a human being with the privilege of language.* And they rolled their eyes in excellent displays of boredom. Your daughter is their age, I believe. Where is she, and who are you to her now? You and I—women—stake our stories in the grass, try to chip away at the self. But the body is a living text, and always has something new to say. ~~Naming me *us*, ropeburn of my shoulder pressed to yours, I take your belonging here hostage.~~ You had a son, a daughter. Somewhere you have a daughter. Language hemorrhages in the petri dish of every sensory frame: *could've been, could've been, could've been.*

Dear P:

A sundial is one of those things I've accepted I'll never understand.
I spend a lot of time in rooms with food in them, and I no longer
believe this to be failure. It's possible that I am some secret, needy
monster you nightmare through your days with. I do not think of you
at all, because I know what you do not: we owe each other nothing. I
haven't given a fake name at Starbucks for months, I no longer speak
like a nest for crickets. Why do we not recognize in liars that seed
which resists eye contact with truth? The secret is how far *never* really
goes, a train hurtling way out past the suburbs, blank plains, flaxen
chigger fields, places trains shouldn't bend to physics. Violence is a
kind of lie, or isn't it? A reconstitution; rewriting the story by force.

Dear P:

I am ashamed of my breast bone, not because it is wide, but because it is wide like my mother's. I fling sand at fleas and watch a Doberman chomp waves, wading out into his joy with the long flank of a black bear. Like joy can swallow, too, if you lose touch with the bottom. After months of nothing, a friend revealed: *My heart is not good*, and I am for days an open window—eschewing "good vibes" and ambiguous healing energy, tumbling baldfaced into prayer when I pass a funeral procession worming along the coastal road through Sopchoppy. There is a part of me that wants to say thank you for giving me this story. When other women ~~(I feel simultaneous the cleaving injustice of this double standard, and only a trickle of shame that I will forgive men almost anything, almost more than anything)~~ are publicly sentimental about their own dead fathers, I am repulsed. And grateful for that. Does it mean I am clear-eyed as shuttles of light swarming across this beach? To love without seeing fully is to love without knowing what it is you love, which is not love at all. I am ashamed of my freckles, my nose in glasses, my genetic bent towards unearned forgiveness. It was not about you: I wanted a second mother like I wanted a new religion, for that novelty glow that lasts a few days. I'm learning if you give some people half a conversation's time, they'll start shooting arrows into an open window out of impulse to lock the shutters on their own.

Dear P:

I have not survived the storylines other people have. My body was never plainly entered without my permission. I fucked someone and my dignity was a hawk nesting without me in inescapable towers. I fucked many someones, my tongue a painted bead, cheap and red and plentiful. The new year was not yet and nothing new. And then it was standing over my bed, shivering like a bracket of train tracks.

Dear P:

My body was never plainly entered without my permission. (Which was
not mine entirely which I begged all day like a child for new frivolous
monumental toy and fled my body once the getting commenced
floated above and made noises to transient bedfellows I'm sure did not
sound like the hauntings they were how was I to know physicality was
not meant to be separate as that tree over there vacillating between
numbness and exceptional raw swells of belonging to a roadside
median a shoetip the evening meaning loneliness was bottomless and
possession began only by lawns sometimes so simple I was allowed to
experience tawny car lights as glorious and exceptionally for me) The
week of the funeral, D assured us that women in the prison where you
live rape each other with broomsticks. This was meant as consolation.

P:

Let me tell you the story of the trees: In another life I abandoned my body before the trees, but this is not about that. I bathed myself and cooked soup which I ate for fearsome hollow my stomach's sake, I cared for myself as one might a turtle cracked by a tire, put myself to bed. But this is not about that either. Young, selfish, inhuman, I sobbed at the thigh of a red oak, let insects chip away irrelevant: *take take*. As if through their hunger I could build erasure out of me. ~~My telling this helps no one.~~ Yes I was addicted to things I was quiet I kept to myself. No one knew, I didn't know what to call it how it broke me mindbody as primal whip breaks feral jaw. ~~How much of me is fractured; what chasms to commodify. My telling this helps no one.~~ Unsatisfied with the tour of pre-made hells I built my own. All my paper men and I their sliming architect. Shifty-eyed. Survival-mouthed. The problem of my hell was how I didn't want to give it away not for anything even a self. ~~How much it's about me, always, makes this not Art. Also not Living; hyperawareness of being is unsustainable without the whiplash of complete un-being.~~ My telling this helps no one. I collect quotes about light messy in notebooks; funnel my hands into a nothing god; watch holiness splatter instantly on any windshield. Truth is, I just built other hells whose walls are quieter, whose stomachs have doors and sometimes I leave them unlocked.

P:

Let me tell you a story called *Being Loved is a Moat We Tunnel Our Hells Around*: I am 25 my stepfather calls me into the bedroom and reflexively I say *Am I in trouble*. Tells me he's bonetired, ready to die, tells me where the will breathes in its iron box and I am relieved ~~Death such a friend, a mutualistic parasitism familiar as a plagiarist study-buddy what sometimes weeps into each other's textbooks to carry home pages of the other's prized tears.~~ Floodguilt squirmy and horrible: when I was small my mom picked the bumps on my arm, fell asleep in our beds, feet sweated—I burned for her to leave, I shoved my little life away from hers entire I'm sorry. Most hours I'm internally that childhood book with the sad donkey's ear barbed to its barn door. What value is there in confession, this or anyone's? ~~I wish I could slink away quiet and do the work, but I am always sticking out my pale tongue to lightning.~~ Your confession rolled like oil from your mouth; the story goes, you called your sister before he was even cold, moments after his caved face sunk to your carpet. The last time I said *I love you* to my own sister, you were witness—was as she stepped down from the witness stand.

Dear Pam:

Once, my father told me the story of a man who drank a gasoline milkshake and puked in the lit fireplace, making ghosts of his three sleeping sisters. He also liked to tell a story about golf balls. What stories did he tell you? I look up and find myself empty on the beach. A black gull shames its velvet mouth toward the sea. ~~Writing the *you* of someone, pulling another into this space, is accusatory shorthand for everything I hold bone-close and distance.~~ Last summer, I was sitting on the patio of a pizzeria upstate when my sister called with vengeance in her voice to relay that you'd been transferred to a minimum security house, gotten *a lesbian haircut.* And how to break such news to our grandmother. Said you were living, she spat, *among people.* When I put down the phone, L remarked: *I've never seen you so stern.* ~~I promise I am capable of compassion for those unlike myself, those who haven't had to cart around a Story or survive much of anything.~~ Grief is bodily, blends the senses, the selves—it's closest to the fabric of poetry itself; it un-makes meaning, draws metaphor into the experience of our bodies as they wrack and wretch around our maypoles of loss. We are all looking for a vessel, a dummy goblet to speak into. Your name is not proof of anything. It does not prove you exist.

Dear Pam:

Aren't we both slipping quietly out of one pocked skin, tiptoed in the cradle dark. Aren't we each the lip of a singular sentence, sewn out of the record. If I was really speaking to you, and not to myself, or grief, or a myriad of the living and dead, I would send you these letters directly. RB writes: *the dead don't have to mourn / inside the living*, and I bloom chills but can't decide if the dead have such agency to mourn, or if we possess ourselves with mourning; if our ghosts are nothing more than altars we swallow and refuse to re-home. I once sent you a letter, an actual one, in the mail; it came back unopened, and I tell people you refused it, but truthfully, I might've just gotten the address wrong. I don't remember its words, only the sentiment: I don't think you are a monster. It is very hard to be a person. And spooling dread inside my chest was fear of how furious my grandmother would be if she read that. You wrote to her, too, slid a letter under her front door days after you killed her son. There is a kind of plea between women in which anything can be made briefly to feel like an apology for spilled coffee, a flipped casserole, a forgotten birthday barbeque. What they see of each of us is an edit—the revised and powdered seams between words, slippery as old scars. I sit here and I sit here, but the sea its own indomitable self, always leaving. ~~I think I asked if you dream about him.~~

Pamela:

Your name implies that once, you were young. You were insightful and calm and found power in that. You spit laughter loud, found power stumbling into complete, unbearable aliveness on a moment's notice. You were probably on a beach, once. Hair whipping streaks across your forehead. K said there's faith required in taking your clothes off with anyone, trusting they won't pull a knife out of their boot, that you won't—or will—get your heart broken, depending on your preference. It's advice the once-young give. I confess to you here, mother of bullets, narrative revolver spun in skin, things I would not to the kind woman who bled me into this world: Tonight, I slept with a man and we kissed and laughed and danced painted in the great river of my blood. The most revelatory freedom can look like love and can also look like violence and be neither. I hope when I'm older, like you, I will have less to say. I hope I let the wind be itself without comment on its qualities. ~~Like you~~ —~~What brand of imprisonment will I confess myself into the arms of? Who might I make corpses of to protect their names from my ledger of abandonment?~~ A craving for language sculpts us into near-deities of carnage. How we climb inside the light of one another to mine our most expensive metaphors.

# V

# SUN COME ANTLERED

## AUGUST, A DECADE OF GRIEF STORIES

All summer I walk in the shade & grow
comfortable being monstrous. Porcelain
as swine, that good dread yawning
between my hips. Like the bitten inside of a cheek,
dead things feel close this month. In June I knew
so many sweetwild rabbits. Once upon a time
every vulture was a blankness. In this age
of Saturn's return, a cardinal is so close
to scarlet tanager it's not even funny, & it's hard
to fight for a self while playing Ambassador of Grief,
fielding diplomatic apologies with flytape.
Women like stories where we get to be our own
unreliable narrators, so I gave my fear sexy names
like *Sunrise* & *Bucktoothed Fool*. I curled
my home in rancid wood, snapped from it
a coronet of colored lights. I was unprepared,
but never stupid. I will think there's something noble
about saying this & there won't be.
In my 25th year I brought people to graveyards
in order to kiss them. It was the only way that made
sense. In this city the glittering lung, we are
what we pretend to forget.

## CHRISTMAS DAY BLACKBLOODED I GET EVERYTHING I WANT

Meaning karma has failed
& I return no venomous
pregnancy narrative spitting
orange at the shattered
horizon Slept in my car

to avoid intimacy with a man
who once sobbed on my belly lifted
my hair in the shower
while I giggling washed
from me his saccharine

pheromone Each minute touching
him new-citied felt a dutiful favor
to younger selves On TV
Illinois is devastated littered
with vagrant wood There are fires

tonight in Paris The president claims
to care about farmers In America's
forgotten earlobe I lack
resolve & cigarettes I desire
to be sentimental

violently Like moths
fucking themselves
against a light fixture
in a rainstorm If there's a pool
table why not lay

your body across it let townies
with sticks enact whatever
they deem justice The lamps
so generous spilling
blue I'm ashamed at my own

craving for myth Woke
in the parking lot parallel
to an old life & mist
pooling the crick in my neck
Friend tells me stories of people took

fingernail scars on their faces
under the weary guise
of livelihood performed
as compassion I ask him teach me
how to destroy something & get

away with it We like to
believe we are sympathetic
villains we can sometimes stare
so hard we forget language
is a sandwich of graves So what

I loved wrong hoof-trampled I folded
like a collapsed star told no one broke
words like plates with my ceramic fists
A man called me by my body I tilted
my jaw to the sky

& laughed out a field of crows

## ADMISSION (AN ARS POETICA)

Once, a toothed-up cupcake on a garbage can's rim, and sitting next to it, the redvelvet carcass of a crow.

Once, I wrote only of trees for two years, devoted days to their various names, branded the prayer of my life in heartwood. Met people and said: *Are we light from the same pine?* Desired people, surrender-palmed, and said: *I come to you a vessel of seeping pith.*

Once, The People existed, and in my head I dollhoused them into one Person. I tried to make love to The People as if I was their devastated paramour and their sepia-tinted train was rounding the edge of the frame, but found myself sap-struck and masturbating in the grass, writhing against the comfortable shadow of an oak.

Once, I abandoned myself over the gray torso of a southern beach. My bellybutton was a single glass hour and there was a starfish in my chest purpling and gasping and losing its limbs all over the place. A Person said: *Promise not to write about this* and I said *Yes* and I fucking lied.

Once, I knew it was my job to listen and translate the light, so I kept mouthing *light, light, light,* hoping The People would understand. I kept trying to describe the light through petals of significant flowers, hollering out to light through my car window as one would a loosed hound, even goddamnit bought the word *light* from a shady internet website. Then the light became noise, like an airplane revving into static, and my mouth was only my mouth. The People got tired and went home, and I went home, and fell asleep on my yellow couch with the light on.

I wrote: *I bought earrings shaped like knives.* I wrote: *We are all trying to find some sideways path to loved.* Some sentences are hostages brandishing the same ropes.

Once, I put on clothes and makeup and shaped my hair into a carnival of acceptability, then walked into a building, sat down in a room, and a Person constricted their vocal chords until they'd built a sound that made sense to human ears, and that sound was the sound of saying it's not useful to tell you, here, how I am bodily like this. Griefwild and keening across the page. Guiltily shoving that *I,* long column of self, down your throat like a hollow-flamed sword.

I admit, the cupcake and its crow are not mine—happened in a distant state whose name is forever the taste of ashy snowslush on a suburban curb.

I admit: I was told our only hope for Art resides in men we've never known, pouring concrete in a state we've never been to. And believed that. I forgot *paper* is a name for the pulp we dismantle from old gods. How we use them to carve eternal our representations of spent fireflies. I forgot when I say *I am revelation,* the *We* is implied. Surely somewhere on this deadening rock, a gathering of pigeons live in perfect satiety. Maybe someday I'll write a poem that doesn't want to tell anyone anything.

## GENEALOGY: LEGUMES

### I

The serrated back of my tongue, the part
I can't reach, is problematic. Thanksgiving,
my mother pirouettes carbs, tells me fat cells
            are like matter: once created never leave
us. What is home? Far
from it, the word of my city sounds
incantation—a sacrilege between the teeth
            of disfavored relatives. This year, the keto diet
declares Christmas dinner ham flank.
On New Year's, there are no black-eyed
peas, their lolling irises staring up from the bowl
            like fetal oracles.

### II

It is difficult to learn an instinct
towards suffering. Only a few of us
become foragers, cleaving
            our hides for a chance at something
fanged & sacred. A friend's mom dies,
leaving her orphaned, & I reach out
before the funeral. Days later she responds:
            *I will be thanking you for your message.* As if
my words haven't arrived through the wires
or been received at the dirt-damp floor of her.
Winter shows up late, wine-drunk
            on its favorite martyred gourd. I consider
*daughter* as noun: a long velvet bow, burgundy
& pearl-sewn. Like sacrament, like a dog's
cone, I knock my head against furniture
            in guilty attempt to slough off the verb.

## III

My grandmother will not replace her 60-year-old
can opener. My mother on Sundays wears
cowboy boots now. My sister's accent thickens
            each time we speak. They whittle
their ribcages with heirloom spoons
as their husbands' costumes outgrow them.
In my childhood home, lima beans
            were forbidden; my stepdad, in his youth,
forced by his own father
to eat them, spit mush into his milk
glass to hide the evidence.
            His father caught on, beat him
for the disobedience. I was enthralled
by those forbidden beans—their electric green
like the painted walls of my staple-scarred bedroom.
            I begged my mom to serve them, & when
she did, my stepfather flung the dinner table.

## IV

After the divorce, my dad cooked us
simple meals, canned: peas, briny artichokes,
succulent, oozing baked beans. That was before
            he marched back into the lunatic cave
of marriage, before he was a construction
of ash. Maybe every woman's heart
is a Freudian clusterfuck; in bed, my sometimes-lover laughs
            slow-motion shutter-frame, transforms
into a sudden child or young father in an old
photograph. It's a kind of childish loss, realizing
the things we can no longer ration our blood to
            solely by virtue of our having bled for them. I hope
someday
to say *love* like it's not a splintered fingernail. When I kiss
him, I rarely anymore notice the roadkill
            aftertaste of uprooting vegetables that so easily know how
to grow upwards from the ground.

## COYOTE

No one talks about February's cruelty,
        a month of rotting figs
that will not acknowledge its flies.

The point of all this living: to preserve
the heart's gentleness, rather than contribute
        to its hardening. So I help you fill

your apartment with green things, but
we darkly know, browsing aisles of fern
        & aloe, we are choosing
what to kill—what eventually wilts

in the stream of days swarming
the sink-bottom. That naming
        a silent thing does not save it, only
twists failure into funeral.

I tell you my theory on vulnerability,
        how it's a history of foliage
shadowing the window above each body
that has passed through mine.

You say it's more the sinkholes
pocketing these craggy rivers, then describe
every round object in the room except the chrome
        terrarium of our breath.

In this dowager night, we take flashlights
        to the abdomen's damp holler.
In mine you find a raccoon with teeth

& one without, each leering at the other
        to make the first move. Meanwhile, a pair
of hungry lanterns fix their sight,

a splinter on the horizon line.
        How I wade through the sawgrass of you,

learning to love equally the coyote
          & what it doesn't yet know
was built to bleed beneath it.

## NASHVILLE YEAR

*for Allison*

remind me the underbelly      our year of suffering      we waded the
dark      in long frayed dresses our backyard moss-rich      branches
bearing scissors      poised for happiness      to drift off the skies like a
sneeze      Allison the heart wants to bolt      toward or away from

> states  away  someone  is  stacking  dishes        muffled
> through the wall      like porcelain organizing        beneath
> skin & considering        not to be lonely        Allison these
> strawberries        never stop coming        terribly sweet alive
> your newborn wraith

pacing winedrunk on the porch      choking on empty jars      of coconut
oil      that year you crawled abandonment      up & down dirt escalators
I assembled an empire of men      to dethrone me from vanishing      we
were grotesque & lucky

> painting sidewalks with our small harmed smiles      grazing
> like a curb the face of god        & eternally cat hair on the
> floor        that year the three hospitals:        wandering halls
> in an orange dress shredded        by the seatbelt's force        I
> didn't cry

until the x-ray nurse asked if I was sure      I couldn't be pregnant I said
*no one has kissed me      in a year* & folded like a sheet      dropped from
singing wire      was made chemical a firefly tunneling robotic wind
then the hit & run the bump        on your forehead the afterwards
midnight milkshakes      that kept you sick for days

> the  spark  drowned        from  your  limbs  dopamine
> withdrawal & the evangelizing nurse        who would not
> help you the Lazarus      in the wheelchair lifting        the
> soiled blanket from      his head in hazy praise      I want
> to reach through the glass

ribcage of the past to tell you     stripped naked face down in the
crumb-littered carpet how     love is the smallest unearthing     a
child's utterance     from the gut of a crypt     Allison next year is so
entirely spring behind the face     I fall asleep nearly giggling     at all
I can have if I only choose it     the story of the future     is that birds
show up clattering at your window     so many-throated you couldn't
name them

       bullets if you tried     your hair was the bridge     between
       hurtling sunlight & the two-     pronged tower     the
       year we lived together a girl flung herself off an overpass
       & no one     reported it on the radio

## *AUBADE WITH FINCHES & NEW MATTRESS*

in the story Thumbelina
feared her body so much she almost married
a mole from the ground      what bureaucracy

we create to keep our hearts inside
their beautiful hells      I wish for love
to be inconsequential      as an oyster unsalting itself

in the gulf      I chose a kind man      I bought
a new mattress      so as to no longer sleep
with bereavement's nectar      but I don't know

how to keep happiness leashed
& my fear is lawless      I want to be
a prettier vector today      to say *o swim*

*in my glass chest glimmering minnow I promise*
*never to boil you*      but dignity is a hearse
snaking the dry pines & in the riverbed

of summer I'm a cemetery of cypress
whittled to toothpicks      snapped off along the road
from the months-ago hurricane      Byron's lover mailed him

a lock of her pubic hair with a note apologizing
coyly for the smear of blood      & I'm embarrassed
to tell my lover I believe in the machinery

of the universe      embarrassed to refer
out loud to anyone as *my lover*      what do you call the person
whose skin you can fall asleep against without feeling

like a drowning victim      a wet wind rolls in
to mop away the street's magnolias      my friend asks which
pair of heels will help them demand Lake Michigan

into spring      I want to be good
at being      so when joy hands me
a fistful of burial      I say *thank you*

*for the temporary* through clenched teeth
I place my skeleton a fish-scale wafer
on the monster's tongue     surrender to the eye

of the holy feared thing     at night my lover uproots my mistakes
from the bed frame     in the morning the finches
are as always     so blathering     someday I will tell him

the story of the fox who leapt
from the balcony ledge & why
I did not follow her

## I SAW THE PARADE OF SNAKEBIRDS & UNDERSTOOD

why people name their children things like *triumph*

I misread *soft pretzel* as *self-portrait*
          The day was otherwise normal

in that I pretended it was     Though
the glory of the day is stillwater

there are honeysellers everywhere
All those trees

who warn their neighbors of bitter
danger & pass electric sighs

through fungi & will so long survive
          us     At night I chew on heart-shaped

sprinkles, ball-shaped sprinkles,
chicken dust     I whittle half a stick

of butter with my unglamorous
front teeth     When the radio says *scarcity*

I think of my mother who would
eat the bones if she could     These long noons

do have wartime vibes     Waking up
to slide into the dread machine

*Who constructs the smaller*
*crane that constructs the crane*

*flies?* someone said shotgun a million
hours ago & I loved him

& I still do     Not for that
          An accident: getting close enough

to smell a stranger's cologne, my lonely
only bones twanged     My stomach tripped

over its own shadow, glories of the day
Glorious birdsong shattering on windowpanes

      Glorious sheet of ochre pollen

pummeling untouched
automobiles     I change my clothes

so the mailwoman isn't frightened
for me when she, ten seconds each

afternoon, speaks between the slats
of the screened porch

Is anticipatory grief not still
               just fucking grief?

Wept glory falling on the brightly pink mimosas

Floridian sun in its great febrile glory

     I am learning to love you in this inside way

Tender unborn beech we will have survived
this in order to know you

Little scarlet-nosed friend

     Little worm that I scrounge beside

## TALLAHASSEE SPRING

I


Passing a rare live deer at the side
of the highway, far enough
in the grass to pretend it doesn't know

the twisted necks & blank eyes its kind
are prone to, a lineage of split livers
ant-eaten like cupcakes

My mother says possums kill
by tunneling up through a creature's ass
*It's true.* Kick a dead calf, a possum
peeks sheepishly out the bloated mouth

Hold my hand ten more miles & I'll stop
myself from telling you, again, about the dead
bird in my Kentucky yard & the other
who landed to stare. Unflinching

Even the rabbits are hiding
long-eared ghosts—someone they swallowed
for safekeeping. What if we chose to forget

the impulsive deployment of knives, if we believed
honeybees were the only blameless beings
The cows like mannequins in their pastures of dark

II


Birds & more birds
plow the bluegray morning
The shivery opulence with which we split
into a nest of hotbreathed animals

Splayed like iguanas in the daylight
Sometimes you are touching me
& I am thinking up ways to get ovened into dirt

Witnesses, too, are actors
in the grieving process. Driving into
Florida's oblong belly, I memorized
new spells for desire: tying hair strands
around a bay leaf, then burying it

with both hands in red mud. If you have someone
who will bury with you, the spell is simply
a symptom of its conditions

Again I lay at your back, wearing
the face of the wolves that ate me

III

When a leaf sprouts does it name itself
Preparation For The Rotting

If you love someone why not make them happy
without you

IV

There is nothing so alive as crying
under purgatorial dawn filtered
through the clanking brogue of a train tunneling backward

Watching briary porches on brick tenements
slide away from us like futures
The whole sweet metal sow, inside its glass stomachs
I grow fat with wonder

How potato chip bags & dogs & daylight are all
made of dark space matter & us too, yes, your finger

hooked through my finger like the tiniest window latch, my heart
clinking between your teeth,
the smallest unlatched window

# V

*I feel dying.* Small children say this
Hothouse as fuck this Tallahassee spring
Slivers of broken lightbulb glittering the bedsheets

There was a woman sleeping in the road
that wraps around the cemetery
A stranger

Green green bottomland
wilding my sorrow
with unrelenting blooms

Let us look on one another
with the joyful urgency of cakebearers

## ARS POETICA AS EULOGY

Does it matter that the dead man's body was discovered
by a fig tree sprouted from a seed
            in his stomach. Or that when I saw
the headline, my mouth cottoned with dread

over how flooded with desire
the burning palms of the internet
            to write about it. At this point in history
everything's a corpse.

Siken writes *seed to flower to fruit to rot*
& knows we are fumbling to sculpt
            a metaphor for death to predate the fact
our metaphors for death have aged bald

& heavy-handed. Nature doesn't need us & neither
do the dead: even ghosts we shackle
            our breath to don't come back
to live inside the worlds we rewrite for them.

Does it matter my conveniently forgetting
the man had been murdered, as my father
            was murdered, a graveless votive
without roots. Or that the man was a victim

of *political violence*, a fire whose horrors
I can't begin to understand in my childlike
            suffering, wracked, wrapped in floral
silk & too much choice. Are we entirely

better people when we erase as much
of ourselves as possible & repurpose
            the deadweight meat as poetry—a language
closer to religion than love? *A hole*

*may have been formed by the explosion*
*allowing light into the dark interior*
            *of the cave. This may have allowed the fig tree*
*to grow inside the body.* Each bright hemorrhage

is incomplete without noticing the floor
buckled beneath it. Every story about grief
            is a story told in reverse: the sea dammed, fireflies
whittling away into their black huts,

our walls given back to the land. Rot to fruit to flower
to seed. You reach into a mouth of soil
                    & feel a branch reaching back.

## MY WISH IS AT LEAST ONCE A WEEK TO FEEL MORE FLAME THAN FLAMMABLE

I hope there is sunlight when I die     Thank you for seeing
whatever is stunning in me & also the trees   This is not so much
one-dimensional happiness as it is the emotional content
of a sunflower     Glorious morning
of coffee & weather     Tongueless ferns
glowing delirious     Steakknife in wooden porchgate
gutted bathtub in the palm ivy yard     Here we shed
our tedious costumes & reclaim
the anarchic confetti laughter     Our modest religion
of beerdrunk swaying
You destitute with joy on your deathbed of light

I've fought like mud suffered animal-pelted to say green
is my favorite color & mean it     To hold eye contact
when you flood red & hazy in the corner
of the goldenplated bar     To speak & have my words
be the opposite of glass     My lungs
are harvest watching the drapes fumble
this torrential beauty   I want the world flushblunt
against my face like newborn animal body heat
All around us creatures are fucking in transit
wildness nuzzling the landscape
into orgasm     The greatest tragedy of living
on this one-mouthed earth is that there are only so many synonyms
for light     I am trying to find new language
for the heavy brightness raining down from nowhere
to free us in our nowhere     Why can't I stop

turning boneless for people who tremble through spacetime
incurring wounds along the way     I'd trade you
a new arm for all your broken     This will not make
any of us whole but it might
make us tilt our petaled eyelids away from the ground
more     Might make us believe for a moment our faces
perfectly seaweed & saltwater     Every structure is a cabana
if you can pin down the water around it     I hope wherever you are
you've eaten pizza & forgotten
the futile necessity of your body     Today I blame

my compassion for what's ravaged
on the moss canopies all this forgiving
navyblue wind but maybe
my heart is simply a garden hose     I do not need to see
a hummingbird to know at any moment we're closer
to a hummingbird than far     I am sweet thighmeat

for mosquitoes in the yards of Gulfport & I'd let them
devour me bonepicked to prolong
this porchsong moment     Today I do not need to feel pretty
to feel pretty     Sitting at this table forged from bluejays
is my greatest accomplishment     One day we will all
be bleeding out of our ears so why not dump the sugar
in the coffeepot insert a laugh
between an openmouthed kiss scream the words
we love most unbearably     I want to drink
orange juice with borrowed vodka     I want to straddle your hips
in the lawn chair of bad decisions     We are lucky
there are stray dogs to sing between
the fenceposts     Let them sing let them

# Notes

"The heart of the warrior is a moon-faced thing" owes itself to Allison Adams, who first shared the "Moon Pose" myth with me. This poem also incorporates information from *Animals Strike Curious Poses* by Elena Passarello, a panel on consent narratives at the 2018 Northeast MLA Conference in Pittsburgh, PA, and various google searches lost now to time.

In "Failed Animals," the anecdote "sack full of cows' tongues" was a gift from Lucy Karam.

"[not these white pills laced with sun]" was inspired by Rebecca Hazleton's book *Fair Copy*, which creates acrostic poems from selected lines of Emily Dickinson poems.

The bell hooks line in "Elegy for Recording the Light" is paraphrased from hooks' book *All About Love: New Visions.*

"These Weeks are Exceedingly Floral" owes itself to Nate Duke, for the ending.

"Ars Poetica as Elegy" references Kamau Brathwaite's poem "Hawk," Richard Siken's poem "Boot Theory," Yolanda Franklin's poem, "White Room Syndrome," a Wikipedia article on the lives and deaths of Mary and Percy Shelley.

In "Holding the Loose Bones Close," "the poet" is Laura McCullough, who writes of burying her children's' teeth in her poem "Possession."

The tiger referenced in "(The Billboard Claims) Caged Tigers Live Longer in Lafayette" was Tony the Tiger, who lived at the Tiger Truck Stop in Grosse Tette, Louisiana until his death in 2017, when he was replaced by a camel.

The epigraph of "At the Locust Fork of the Black Warrior River" refers to House Bill 314 passed in Alabama in May 2019, and a similar bill proposed in Georgia the same year, which aimed to impose a near-total ban on abortion state-wide.

# NOTES

"I saw the parade of snakebirds & understood" was written in April 2020, during the first weeks of the COVID-19 pandemic, in which various media sources used the term "anticipatory grief" to describe our collective experience.

In "Gulf Epistolary" the quote "the dead don't have to mourn / inside the living" is from Ruth Baumann's poetry collection *Parse*.

"Ars Poetica as Eulogy" was inspired by, and quotes a line from, a 2018 viral article which describes a man's body found after a fig seed that was in his stomach when he died sprouted a tree. It references Richard Siken's poem "Love Song of the Square Root of Negative One."

The italicized line in "Late September Early October Hemorrhage" is a lyric from Lucy Dacus' song "Nonbelievers."

# ACKNOWLEDGEMENTS

This book is for my family. Thank you for your support and love.

This book is for Lena Ziegler, my sweet and unmatched ideal reader, and for CJ Scruton, Allison Adams, Clinton Craig, and Cameron Moreno—my writing family forever.

This book is for my Tallahassee friends and beloveds, who are all over these pages: John Oldenborg, Nate Duke, Nick Bon, Collin Callahan, Diamond Forde, Andrew Zolot, Zach Linge, Nathan Mullins, Damian Caudill, Lindsey Hugen, and my Cohort Coven: Brett Hanley, Lauren Howton, Bridget Adams, Rebecca Orchard, and Keri Miller. Thank you for surviving Florida (and multiple natural disasters) with me.

This book is for my teachers and mentors: Lindsey Eckert, David Kirby, Barbara Hamby, Skip Horack, Mark Winegardner, Aline Kalbian, and David Bell, who were kind when I needed it.

This book is for my students, who remind me why any of this matters.

This book is for Florida State University, the Woodstock Byrdcliffe Guild, and PEN America, who gave me time, support, community, and beauty.

This book is for Jenny Irish and Tanya Grae, two poets I admire deeply, who were kind enough to provide beautiful words about this collection in addition to their mentorship and friendship.

This book is for Alex Howard, who loaned me "Marilyn," on which this and two other manuscripts came to life.

This book is for my agent, Cassie Mannes Murray, who has been a tireless cheerleader through disappointments, triumphs, and a literal pandemic, and is an overall awesome human being.

This book is for Leza and Christoph at CLASH, who believed in it, made it beautiful, and shepherded it into the world.

This book is for The Bark, Waterworks, The Wilbury, Leon Pub, and even fucking Fire Betty's.

This book is for Banjo Bones and Amelia Goose, who offer their bellies freely, as if everyone deserves it.

This book is for Tallahassee, and for the trees.

This book is for you: suffering, glorious, alive—I hope you let yourself feel it all.

# ᴀCKNOWLEDGEMENTS

Grateful acknowledgement is given to the following publications where these poems first appeared, some in different forms:

*Bayou Magazine:* "Nashville Year"
*Birdcoat Quarterly:* "[River]"
*Black Warrior Review*: "Gulf Epistolary"
*Cincinnati Review*: "No Horses"
*Entropy:* "Holding the Loose Bones Close" & "(The Billboard Claims) Caged Tigers Live Longer in Lafayette"
*Gigantic Sequins:* "Ars Poetica as Elegy"
*Hayden's Ferry Review*: "My Wish is At Least Once a Week to Feel More Flame Than Flammable"
*Hobart*: "I Hope My Salt Lamp is a Weeping Deity"
*The Journal*: "Coyote"
*Matador Review*: "Christmas Day Blackblooded I Get Everything I Want"
*Michigan Quarterly Review*: "At the Locust Fork of the Black Warrior River"
*Muzzle Magazine*: "Aubade with Finches & New Mattress"
*New South*: "How We Reckon"
*NightBlock*: "Inevitably you will know people" & "Splinterwood Solstice"
*Pandemic Publications*: "I saw the parade of snakebirds & understood"
*PANK*: "Failed Animals"
*The Florida Review*: "Elegy for Recording the Light" & "Tallahassee Spring"
*The Pinch*: "These Weeks are Exceedingly Floral"
*The Rumpus*: "The heart of the warrior is a moon-faced thing"
*The Seventh Wave:* "Inheritance" & "The Beekeeper's Abortion"
*Split Lip Magazine*: "Notes on Un-Apology"
*Tammy:* "The Cool Girl Façade Begets its Own Layer of Animal Grief"
*Tinderbox Poetry Journal:* "Late September Early October Hemorrhage"
*TYPO:* "[not these white pills laced with sun]"

A selection of these poems appeared in the *Oxidant | Engine* Box Set Series Volume 3, under the title *Land of the Floral & Rootfisted.*

# Erin Slaughter

Erin Slaughter is the author of *A Manual for How to Love Us,* a debut short story collection forthcoming from Harper Perennial in 2023, and two books of poetry: *The Sorrow Festival* (CLASH Books, 2022) and *I Will Tell This Story to the Sun Until You Remember That You Are the Sun* (New Rivers Press, 2019). She is editor/co-founder of *The Hunger,* and her writing has appeared in *Black Warrior Review, CRAFT, Slice, Prairie Schooner,* and elsewhere. Originally from Texas, she is a PhD candidate at Florida State University, where she co-hosts the Jerome Stern Reading Series. Find her online at erin-slaughter.com

# ALSO BY CLASH BOOKS

GAG REFLEX
Elle Nash

WHAT ARE YOU
Lindsay Lerman

PSYCHROS
Charlene Elsby

AT SEA
Aïcha Martine Thiam

THE SMALLEST OF BONES
Holly Lyn Walrath

AN EXHALATION OF DEAD THINGS
Savannah Slone

WATERFALL GIRLS
Kimberly White

ALL THE PLACES I WISH I DIED
Crystal Stone

LIFE OF THE PARTY
Tea Hacic-Vlahovic

GIRL LIKE A BOMB
Autumn Christian

THE ELVIS MACHINE
Kim Vodicka

WE PUT THE LIT IN LITERARY
**clashbooks.com**

 @clashbooks   @clashbooks   /clashbooks

*Email*
clashmediabooks@gmail.com